The Public Library
REPORTER

NUMBER 16

Community Service

Innovations in Outreach
at the Brooklyn Public Library

Compiled and edited by

Dorothy Nyren

Coordinator of Adult Services
Brooklyn Public Library

AMERICAN LIBRARY ASSOCIATION

CHICAGO, 1970

International Standard Book Number 0-8389-3117-0 (1970)

Library of Congress Catalog Card Number 77-137361

Copyright © 1970 by the American Library Association

All rights reserved. No part of this publication may be reproduced in any form without permission in writing from the publisher, except by a reviewer who may quote brief passages in a review.

Printed in the United States of America

Contents

Introduction Dorothy Nyren	1
Reaching Out—With a Full, Not an Empty, Hand! Doris Bass	4
Reviewing the Rules John Gettys	11
Film Service to the Community Thalia-Manon Tissot	17
A Changing Library for a Changing Neighborhood Marilyn Chandler	24
The Coney Island Community: A Case Study Martin Lubin	31
Ask the People—They Know Where It Is Addie Powell	39
The Community Coordinator Program Thelma Black	43
The Bushwick Branch Bash Bessie Bullock	51

Appendix
    Materials Selection Policy of the
    Brooklyn Public Library
	55

Introduction

Dorothy Nyren
Coordinator of Adult Services
Brooklyn Public Library

Brooklyn is the biggest borough of the biggest city of the Western Hemisphere. Brooklyn has far more Jews than Tel Aviv and enough Italians and Irish to populate full-size cities. It has a mix of many other national groups: Germans, Poles, Scandinavians, Russians, and even Arabs and Mohawk Indians. What it lacks conspicuously is the majority group in America—white Anglo-Saxon Protestants. In the last few decades the black and Puerto Rican population of Brooklyn has grown to approximately 20-30 percent of the total. The most recent ethnic influx has been the French-speaking natives of Haiti.

Brooklyn has escaped the more violent ethnic confrontations that have been eroding the stability of American cities, but her relative peace is an uneasy condition, liable to disturbance at any moment. To cope with the diversity of the population it serves, to keep from being ossified to an institutional old age and solidified into a monument to be observed rather than used, it has been necessary for the Brooklyn Public Library to learn how to respond to the variant and constantly shifting needs and desires of the peoples of Brooklyn.

As John C. Frantz, former director of the Brooklyn Public Library,[1] said at a hearing conducted by the Metropolitan Area Library Service Committee of the Public Library Association in 1967:

---

[1] In May 1970, Mr. Frantz became Executive Chairman of the National Book Committee, and Mr. Kenneth F. Duchac succeeded him as director of the Brooklyn Public Library.

The question is the extent to which librarians should attempt to convert non-users into users on the one hand, or attempt to convert the library into a different, more responsive institution. This is not offered as an either/or choice. The operative word here is <u>extent</u>.

Assuming that the public library has a pretty useful product, as we think it has, we have to convince those who don't use it that it is useful to them. On the other hand, how much of our product really isn't useful to people who don't use it? To the extent that is true, we have to change our product to meet new needs. I think it is identifying the mix of these two approaches that may be very helpful in making libraries, books, and library services more relevant to people who, I am convinced, are unaware that they need these services, or do not know how to obtain them.

I am struck by the fact that where we have conventional library facilities in neighborhoods which they were designed to serve, we are doing a very good job. In other words, where we are operating a conventional library for conventional library users, we are doing an excellent job. But where we are trying to give that kind of library service to a radically different kind of user, we are doing a poor job.[2]

The practical job that librarians are in the process of trying to accomplish is to determine where and when traditional library service is the best library service and to what degree and in what local units some sorts of nontraditional materials and facilities may be added or substituted. To that end a variety of approaches has been tried. Fundamental to all of them is an open-minded experimental attitude, a willingness to listen to suggestions from the total range of staff and patrons, and the realization that some percentage of nonsuccesses must be accepted as an inevitable part of innovation. Development of staff initiative and an increase in the opportunities that local staff are given to make local decisions are basic to an increase in differentiation between units and a resultant improved matching of community interests and the library's ability to function in relation to these interests.

As John Gettys reports in his paper, "Reviewing the Rules," an overhaul of all library regulations toward the end of making them more flexible and accommodating to the public interest

---

[2] Judith D. Guthman, ed., <u>Metropolitan Libraries: The Challenge and the Promise</u>, Public Library Reporter, no.15 (Chicago: American Library Assn., 1969), p.27-28.

was a first step in improving community service. Simultaneously the Book Selection Policy was revised to a Materials Selection Policy, whose major goal was to keep the library's options open and make it possible to reach out, as Doris Bass explains, "with a full, not an empty, hand." The role of the Audiovisual Department has been expanded and continues to grow. Thalia-Manon Tissot explains some of the ways in which film can be used in outreach activities.

Within the framework of new attitudes and new materials, most progress has been made by individual initiative with the library administration's chief role being to free staff members for innovation and to offer support to their efforts. Branch librarians have had much to contribute, particularly in making contacts with local organizations and offering library support to local activities. Martin Lubin in "The Coney Island Community: A Case Study" describes a most successful instance of this type of community involvement. Other branch librarians have radically altered the atmosphere and holdings of their units; Marilyn Chandler's "A Changing Library for a Changing Neighborhood" reports on that process.

In other parts of Brooklyn a district plan has been put into operation. Administrative and professional staff for a group of four or five units is centralized in the largest library. Materials selection and programming for the small community libraries are performed by specialists at the district level. This makes for maximum utilization of the skills and a greater flexibility in the working schedules of specialists. Addie Powell, a district adult services specialist, tells in "Ask the People—They Know Where It Is" how a specialist can serve varied ethnic groups in a housing project area.

The experimental project for which the Brooklyn Public Library is best known is the community coordinator program. Community coordinators are freed completely from in-library service and are attached to areas rather than to specific buildings. Their whole work has been to interpret the library to the community and the community to the library. Two of the community coordinators report on their activities in this publication: Thelma Black and Bessie Bullock.

The Brooklyn Public Library still has a long way to go in learning how to listen to the voices of its people and how to translate a desire to respond into effective service; nevertheless, progress is being made and modes of adaptation are being evolved. What is being done on a large scale in Brooklyn can be done—probably even more effectively—on a small scale in other libraries in other communities. First one decides to listen; anything may follow.

Reaching Out—With a Full, Not an Empty, Hand!

Doris Bass
Assistant Coordinator of Adult Services
and Director of Youth Services

In 1967 a committee of twelve librarians was appointed to revise the Book Selection Policy of the Brooklyn Public Library. The factors making such revision urgent were stated by the director: the changing population of the borough; increased and altered educational patterns and requirements; and the progress of technology which not only increased the amount of information available, but also the media to which libraries had access. I served as chairman of that committee. On a subjective level, what we hoped to respond to was the feeling of many librarians that we were severely handicapped in our attempts to work with and in our communities by collections that were inadequate for current requirements and by rigid standards and procedures that made it difficult to respond quickly to recognizable needs. Especially among those of us who were working in disadvantaged areas there was an awareness that unless we did something quickly to relate our services to the community, we might just as well fold our tents and quietly steal away—and we would hardly be missed! Declining circulation was a measurable indication of the library's declining vitality, but more important was the sure knowledge that we, as librarians, were not doing what we should be to help find solutions for the enormous problems facing communities in transition and turmoil.

Public libraries had dedicated themselves for so long to such high standards of quality and balance that librarians sometimes lost sight of the elementary fact that it was not possible to evaluate materials apart from a consideration of the potential user. As long as our public was highly literate and book-oriented, we were able to provide effective service. When conflict arose between our standards and patron requirements, we frequently opted in favor of so-called fiscal responsibility (using public money to purchase high-quality materials) rather than in favor of patron responsibility. Brooklyn's new Materials Selection Policy stresses the building of collections based on quality and <u>relevance</u>, with the unspoken recognition that an unused collection, no matter how "good," cannot achieve our primary purposes.

The new policy, which was adopted by the Board of Trustees early in 1969, never uses the word "outreach," but it articulates the same philosophy and hopefully provides support for each agency within the borough and a basis upon which it can turn itself into a real community library. It focuses on the need for agency collections and services which are relevant to their particular neighborhoods, which reflect the totality of needs in the community, and which are responsive to changing needs as they occur, not years after the fact. It stresses the need to integrate all media into the services of the library and provides standards for the evaluation of materials which apply to all media. More important than any of the individual sections within it, the policy expresses an attitude of active involvement with our patrons (actual and potential), and it offers a more broad-minded, flexible approach to selection which permits professionals greater freedom in choosing both the kind and the content of materials for their agency collections.

Formulating a policy is merely a first step—putting it into effect in a system as large and varied as Brooklyn's requires effort on many levels. One might realize that an agency's collection is virtually unused (perhaps even unusable within the context of "reaching out" to the community), but how does one go about making a major change in a short time? On a policy level we wrote in a statement that public demand must be a factor in selection, occasionally superseding stated criteria for selection and best measured by the persons responsible for selection in each agency. On a procedural level, provisions were made for the reevaluation of formerly rejected titles, and formerly hidden books were made available to any agency requesting them. On a practical level, however, it has been the availability of paperbacks and the administrative decision to allow their purchase from a central fund, rather than from individual agency book budgets, which have served most effectively in bringing us closer to the goals stated in the policy. For fifteen months paperbacks have been purchased in massive quantities from this central fund, and the positive results can now be judged.

Paperbacks have served several purposes. They are inexpensive, so we have been able to provide ephemera, student requirements, and other mass demands in quantity, while continuing to build quality hard-cover collections. This means that for the first time we do not have to choose between service to different segments of the community. Paperbacks do not have to be processed, so we can provide materials in demand quickly. They are light in weight, convenient to handle, and expendable (as compared to hard-cover books), so we can take them out into the community without depleting standard collections and with a minimum of physical effort and expense. Most important of all, the great variety of titles allows individual agencies to build specific-interest collections with creative groupings and displays designed to meet the needs and tastes of their particular areas. These "special" collections vary according to the agency's location and go far toward making the library really a part of, and responsive to, its community.

Although paperbacks are being used in the above ways all over Brooklyn, it is in the inner-city areas that they have made the greatest difference in service. As neighborhoods shifted and the library-oriented middle class moved out, we were totally unprepared to meet the needs of our new neighbors. Agencies in such areas were, in truth, "Carnegie Culture Castles." They stood almost as citadels of silence—filled not with people but with dust-gathering books. The majority of people now living in these areas had no contact with, or realization of, the services of the library, and for the few who did come in, the experience was frequently a frustrating one. The shelves were filled with good books chosen to meet standards of merit and balance, but almost meaningless in terms of their lives and life-styles. The adults might keep sending their children in, but rarely did they make return visits. What we had to do, therefore, was to introduce ourselves to the community by going where the people were with what they wanted and needed and to present to them, when they came into the library, collections which were immediately recognizable as being meaningful to them.

Small agencies, with low circulation and consequently small book budgets, were most often the ones which required the greatest overhauling. Our fifteen-month centralized paperback fund has permitted such agencies, for the first time, to purchase what they need in the quantities they need and to reestablish their connection with their communities. Larger

Reaching Out—With a Full, Not an Empty, Hand! 7

agencies, similarly, have been able to meet demands heretofore impossible. We have been free during this period to think, not in terms of merit versus demand, but in terms of "what" and "how many." Now the well has run dry, and we must once again purchase all books from agency budgets. But in this short period of time we have been able to alter radically the content of some collections, to modify others, and, in some cases, just to provide an attractive face-lift. The general rise in circulation throughout Brooklyn during the past few months may be only coincidence, but it may well be a sign that the Brooklyn behemoth hasn't run out of steam and is returning to the vigor of its previous days.

Getting down to specifics, just what have we done with our paperbacks?

1. In more cases than can be counted, our first-time patrons are requesting either ethnic-interest or self-help titles. A few years ago a small agency couldn't cope to provide more than one or two copies of <u>Manchild in the Promised Land</u> or <u>Soul on Ice</u> or a specific Arco title. Today, where they are in demand, one can find from 30 to 100 copies of these titles in paper bindings.
2. In those areas of Brooklyn where the population is heavily Puerto Rican, agencies have large collections of light romances and good nonfiction (including self-help titles) in Spanish.
3. To satisfy the constant demands of our formerly insatiable mystery readers, we finally have enough titles to keep even the most avid fan content, even in agencies whose book budgets were too small to permit wide variety before.
4. Agencies in areas where the demand for best sellers is heavy also have more freedom to keep their housewives happy. Where such pressure is heavy, other less important needs can be met with paperbacks, since the variety of good titles available in paper is great.
5. Throughout the borough there is the great satisfaction of being able to hand students the titles on their reading lists, rather than handing them a note to their teachers absolving the library of responsibility in providing mass-assignment material.
6. In some areas librarians are going out into the community with shoeboxes filled with paperbacks. The boxes are placed in clinics, grocery stores, laundro-

mats—any place where people congregate can become an agency of the library.
7. For years we have invited adult education classes to the library for visits, but we were never able to provide whole classes with the type of books they requested, and the number of return visits from individuals in these groups was small. Now we are able to give them the dictionaries, the baby-care, grammar, and spelling books they ask for, which is a relief for the librarian and surely a requirement for successful outreach.

This past year and a half has seen not only a massive purchase of paperbacks but also a change in the traditional ways in which we view, and consequently use, other materials. Periodical collections in each agency have most frequently been seen in terms of their usefulness for the student and for the browser. Toward the goal of developing true community libraries, we have turned our attention to ways in which this part of our collections can be made more representative of and responsive to our patrons. Not only are we purchasing many titles in heavier duplication (to allow for the circulation of current issues of popular magazines), but we have also permitted individual agencies to select from a much wider range of periodicals than has ever been available before.

To a large extent libraries in the past have avoided the new, the far-out, and the amateur publications whose life span is dubious and whose viewpoint may be questionable. In doing so we have totally neglected the very journals in which the young, the unrecognized talent, and the socially committed are writing. If high school students can't read the <u>High School Free Press</u> and Black Muslims can't read <u>Muhammad Speaks</u> and militants can't read the <u>Black Panther</u> or <u>Rat</u> or <u>The Guardian</u> inside the library, then how can we convince them that we really do want to serve them? This year's periodical list included a large number of radical and reactionary newspapers and magazines as well as several journals of poetry, literature, and opinion whose format may not be professional, but whose content has meaning for the individuals and groups who constitute our public.

One of the most important aspects of the new Materials Selection Policy is its recognition that we live in a multimedia world and that libraries must stop attaching second-class status to audiovisual materials if we are really to do our job. There are too many people who do not respond to books, and too many subjects which films treat more effectively than books, and too many areas in which learning is best accomplished through the combined use of film and print for us to limit ourselves to simply one or two media. Although the whole area of selection and utilization of audiovisual media is complex and filled with as yet unsolved problems for libraries, it is within this area that some of our most pressing service problems will be solved.

Within the Materials Selection Policy is the implicit acknowledgment that our borrowers should have access to the information they need in the form which they can best utilize. To hand a patron a book on the subject simply because the book happens to be on the shelf, and without any consideration of whether or not there is a more effective presentation in another format, is to fool ourselves that we are doing a good job. Our motto used to be: "The right book for the right person"; today we must think in terms of the right material regardless of form.

Brooklyn, like most public libraries, is still far from this goal. The lack of enough projectors, screens, phonographs, and the like; the need to train staff in the selection and utilization of nonbook materials; the need to develop adequate audiovisual collections—all are hurdles to overcome. Because it took us so long to accept audiovisual materials even in the most limited fashion and because of the difficulties involved in integrating newer media into existing book collections, the kind of service the new policy envisions is not just around the corner. We must still "book" films, projectors, records, and phonographs weeks or months in advance for special programs. There is, however, even within such limitations, much experimental work being done with film use in the library, and the future is brighter because of the body of librarians dedicated to finding creative ways to fulfill their functions. We look forward to the time when each agency will have its own audiovisual equipment and small, rotating collections of films and records so that these materials can be used as spontaneously as books currently are for those who come to us for information, for entertainment, or for relief from the pressures of their lives.

The Materials Selection Policy is a statement oriented toward lowering barriers. Within the policy there is no separation according to age groups. The same standards are seen to be applicable to the selection of materials for children, young adults, and adults. The kind of service envisioned depends on the librarian's ability to analyze the patron's requirements, not according to preconceived notions based merely on age, but on an intelligent evaluation of the person and the request, and access to the largest possible body of material. In the same way, the policy does not separate materials according to form; it considers printed and audiovisual materials in terms of which is best for particular tasks, not which is primary or secondary. In attempting to open the whole selection process, to make it more broad-minded, and to relate it more directly to the people we serve, perhaps we shall be able to lower the final barrier—the one which for too long has stood between "us" as a formidable institution and our communities.

Reviewing the Rules

John Gettys
District Librarian
New Utrecht District Library

When the Brooklyn Public Library Procedures Committee (PROCOM) was established in September of 1968, John C. Frantz, who was then director, charged the committee with responsibilities which grew out of the Brooklyn Public Library Board of Trustees' Position Paper, published in April of 1968. He indicated that the paper

> reflects the concern of the library for maximum utilization of its resources in view of rapid and severe changes in our urban environment. To meet these changing situations, the paper calls for reexamination of our traditional patterns and concepts of service to the community of Brooklyn. To be effective in serving the needs of the community the library must be flexible and adaptable to the changing demands of the community it serves. It is also essential to maintain those standards which will assure quality of service and advance the basic objectives of the public library.
>
> The charge to this special staff committee is to examine the existing rules, regulations, practices, procedures, and precedents of the Brooklyn Public Library as they relate to public service operations. This review should then be used as the basis for drafting specific recommendations identifying the practices which should be changed, the nature of the changes required, and the essential reason therefor. In general, initiative and imagination by all staff is to be encouraged so that the capacity of the library to

respond to the community is not unnecessarily inhibited by red tape, obsolete concepts, or bureaucratic methods.

The ten members of the Procedures Committee were selected to provide a broad cross section of experience in public service positions in just as wide a variety of borough neighborhoods. As a general working plan, it was decided to review each policy and procedure, submit preliminary recommendations to Mr. Frantz, and at the same time distribute the recommendations to the general staff for comment. After a careful study of the comments and reactions from staff, a final set of recommendations reflecting any change in the committee's thinking would be prepared and submitted to Mr. Frantz for his approval and subsequent consideration by the Board of Trustees.

While this method turned out to be so time-consuming that in the committee's first year only two procedures ("Meeting Rooms" and "Public Bulletin Boards") passed through all the steps necessary to become official new procedures, the involvement of general staff played a very important part in the work of the committee, and the unanimous opinion of PROCOM is that the benefits of this involvement warranted the time spent in preparation of materials for distribution, evaluation of comments, and revision of recommendations. There is no question that the resulting recommendations are sounder and have much stronger staff support than would have been the case had the committee worked alone.

Although PROCOM made recommendations on a number of aspects of public service during the year, most of the work was concentrated on the two completed procedures and two others ("Registration" and "Fines and Charges") which are awaiting approval by the director. The following comments on these four procedures will illustrate the type of changes members of PROCOM believe need to be made as the first step in developing library procedures which are more responsive to individual community needs.

MEETING ROOMS

The regulations governing use of library meeting rooms had limited use to groups having elected officers, and these groups were required to submit in duplicate a detailed form to be forwarded to the main library for approval. Applicants who seemed to qualify were given a list of requirements and prohibitions which—among other things—prohibited smoking, eating, and advertising the program in the library. Except when the library cosponsored the program, all meeting-room users were charged a fee. Excluded from use of the rooms were teachers or other groups associated with the Board of Education and those who wished to use the room as a classroom or for programs involving physical activity.

The major changes in regulations resulting from the committee recommendations include:

> Shifting of responsibility for approval of meeting from top-level administration to local agency head. This provides the applicant with an immediate answer and makes meetings on short notice possible

> Making rooms available for all meetings except those conducted for personal gain or commercial purposes, and those which present physical hazard to participants or audience

> Simplification of form to be submitted and requirement of only one copy

> Authorization to grant permission for meeting-room use to loosely organized groups or groups in the process of organizing

> Authorization to agency heads to approve smoking, serving of refreshments, and posting of notices advertising meetings held in library

> Elimination of fee for meetings beginning and ending during hours agency is open to public.

In addition to these and other changes, staff members are being encouraged to advertise the fact that the meeting rooms are available and take other steps to stimulate their use. The main unresolved problem in this area concerns charging of fees for any meeting which requires that the custodian change his schedule or work extra hours to keep the building open for the meeting. PROCOM has recommended that steps be taken to eliminate completely fees for use of the meeting rooms. Although this is not possible at present because of lack of funds, it has been recommended as a goal and is considered particularly important for low-income neighborhoods having groups in the process of organizing, since such groups often find it difficult to pay for meeting space.

14   John Gettys

PUBLIC BULLETIN BOARDS

Review of the policy governing bulletin boards revealed regulations which required that most materials be routed through the Public Relations office for approval; that notices showing an admission charge be eliminated; that anything lacking neatness and attractiveness not be posted; that priority be given to notices from cultural institutions and federal, state, and city agencies.

The most important change here shifted approval responsibility from the Public Relations department to the local agency head. PROCOM members believe that the local administrator is in a better position to judge the relative importance of notices to a particular community and would be more inclined to give weight to the message rather than to neatness, artwork, and prestige of the advertising institution. This change in emphasis should result in the posting of many more notices about local activities and strengthen the relationship between library agency and community.

To assist the agency head, some restrictions were retained (anonymous notices, commercial advertising, notices of religious services, notices from political parties), but anything else may be posted and the agency head is the sole judge of its interest and importance to the community. As an additional service to the community, agencies are authorized to maintain a Community Notice Board, on which individuals may advertise personal services for hire and/or personal goods for sale.

REGISTRATION, AND FINES AND CHARGES

In an effort to give the procedures concerning registration, and fines and charges, a more positive tone, recommendations were aimed at emphasizing service and deemphasizing maintenance of delinquency records, withholding of library cards, and penalizing in general. Members of PROCOM agreed that instead of reforming the chronic delinquent, stringent rules and regulations more often serve to penalize the honest borrower who admits responsibility or to intimidate children and underprivileged borrowers.

Main recommendations in these areas include:

Stressing in the training of both clerical and professional staff the importance of flexibility and use of common sense in applications of library rules—particularly in the handling of registration and fines, where the possibility is strong for alienating rather than serving borrowers

Inaugurating the new regulations with an Amnesty Week, during which library materials could be returned with no questions asked and all delinquency records cleared so that every borrower could begin with a clear record

Abolition of all overdue fines for children, reduction in amounts charged for lost children's books, and no curtailing of children's borrowing privileges because of unreturned materials

Retention of the fine system for adults (for present), but general reduction in scale of fines and elimination of overdue charges for Sundays and holidays

Development of a "one-library-card" system, which is in line with the open-access-to-collection policy already in effect

Abolition of identification requirements for children and simplification of those for adults

Immediate issuing of library cards to children below 7th grade; mailing of cards to all adult borrowers having clear records

No charge for duplicate or temporary cards for borrowers who have lost or forgotten to bring their library cards

Use of strong positive approach in all communications with borrowers concerning overdue or lost materials, with emphasis on concern for other borrowers who need materials, rather than on penalties and legal procedures.

Although improving service to the public has been the primary goal in all the recommendations made by PROCOM, of necessity consideration also has been given to the ability of the system to respond to public needs within present staffing patterns and budgetary allowances. To have done otherwise would have delayed the possibility of change to the distant future, considering the length of time required to effect staff and budget changes in any agency of the City of New York. There is no question, however, that a top-to-bottom reexamination of the staff organizational plan is needed, as well as a complete reevaluation of service, particularly in agencies which are a part of a district complex (approximately one-half of the system, with plans for expansion). While this type of activity is outside the scope of PROCOM, recommendations were made concerning the need for such studies.

There is also no question that staff attitudes and training are really much more important than written procedures, since any procedure can work against the public and the library when applied too rigidly or dogmatically. For this reason members of PROCOM have repeatedly emphasized the need for training of staff to use judgment, flexibility, and common sense in dealing with the public—no matter what the procedure involved. The committee is particularly concerned about those supervisors who tend to be more rigid than the staff members working under them, especially since placing more decision-making responsibility on the local level may in such cases work to the detriment of the library and the public. All this points to the need for a complete change in emphasis and attitude before a simple changing of procedures can mean very much. Members of PROCOM feel that they have done a small part in getting the reassessment started, but that the hard work of making the new procedures work as intended still lies ahead.

Film Service to the Community

Thalia-Manon Tissot
Children's Librarian
Crown Heights Branch

When librarians get in a panic from dropping circulation and low attendance at traditional meetings, i.e., book discussions and story hours, they cast around for a new feature to arouse community interest. The answer—a film program! Results? Sure! But not for the reasons most of us assume.

A film program is not a novelty or a frivolous entertainment. Nor should film be regarded as an "easy" approach to learning and a poor substitute for books. Try a film series with the sole purpose of attraction, and it will probably be unsuccessful. Try films because they provide material on subjects of interest to your group, and there should be acceptance.

The Kensington Branch, serving a middle-class area whose residents have a predominantly Jewish and Italian heritage, has slight attendance at its films. How do you account for the standing-room-only attendance by older people when a film on Israel was shown? Or the solid attendance of the teens when drug-use films or the Young Film Makers series were shown? Why was the slide show of Brooklyn scenes by a local citizen so well received?

Film is a communicative art and as such has a legitimate and equal place with print media in library service. While some libraries with more traditional book-oriented patrons have yet to feel the demand for film collections, the advance of film technology and inexpensive projectors, cartridge films, and the like, will eventually create the greatest demand from this middle-class audience. We are just beginning to hear from the first generation that has grown up with television as a household necessity—and thus, to a large extent, films! Nevertheless, it is true that people who do not put a high priority on the print media because of bilingual problems, lack of incentive, little opportunity for formal schooling, or whatever have found film a particularly meaningful communicator for them.

To most of the general population the library has become synonymous with print, and only the most aware patron realizes how many more services are available. Therefore the problem is how to advise our new multimedia generation and our nonprint public that we provide services in their fields of interest and that one of these services is film. This is true film "outreach"—not as a lever for circulation but as an end in itself.

Spreading the word so that it reaches the channels where films are best received is the keystone of service. Since films are generally used inside that conservative edifice dedicated to books, how can you get people through the doors? Take the film out to the people! One method is the street show where a movie is shown on a rear projection screen from a van. The New Lots Branch had summer twilight shows in their concretized back-of-building area—a good remedy for extreme heat, poor projection facilities, and a formal library atmosphere. The availability of a small, automatic, cartridge projector has made it possible for the Crown Heights Branch to include an on-the-spot film show in its plans for a "welcome" party at a new low-income housing development. As there are no reels, threading, or rewinding, it makes film showing hazardless even in the midst of a milling group.

The auditory and direct person-to-person approach is the most effective means of spreading the word in a nonprint-oriented community. Even a mod poster may be admired for its design, yet go unread. Posters in the library will attract only library users, and few borrowers really look around them. One branch has posted its current program information on a stand and placed this directly inside its doors. One must glance at it even if just to avoid tripping.

Posting the notices in outside agencies and stores does put the material where it can be seen by other than library habitués, but, again, how often are they read? Posters covered with saran were posted on an exterior bulletin board in a small park that senior citizens frequented—a novel approach for attracting a specific group.

Flyers are somewhat better received as they carry some of the personal approach. Delivered door-to-door they get where they're needed. Handed out by teachers they carry the seal of an educator's approval. They are most effective when given out personally with a few words exchanged. One library whose building was off the beaten track effectively advertised its film program by handing out schedules in conjunction with a paperback display at the subway during the evening rush hour. Balloons and the more expensive buttons given out at a program can be a type of flyer as inquisitive children ask those filtering back into the community, "How come?" and "Where from?" Again a personal contact!

An exception to the unread printed notice are those ads which saturate a large area—generally in a form not financially possible for the average library. This past summer, remarkable attendance and inquiry about our events for children came in response to a newspaper ad placed as a public service by a department store. Abraham & Straus ran a detailed calendar of all museum, park, and library community events, and the library's branches found people from outside their communities responding. Other library systems might find assistance of this type the answer to lack of advertising funds. They also might find radio spots available as a community service from the local station.

Despite saturation advertising no film program will be attended unless it fills a need felt by the consumer. Contacting organized groups is a beginning to finding out what you can supply to fill their needs. Sometimes a group specifically asks for service as did Phoenix House, a center for rehabilitating drug addicts in Coney Island. The Coney Island Branch informally shows films on topics other than drugs as requested by members of that organization and often has attendance as high as forty.

But sometimes groups are unaware that films are the service that would best suit them. Roberta Levine, at Borough Park, was asked to provide a library program for a group of retarded young adults attending local classes which prepared them for functioning in the outside world. The stories and picture books did not hold their interest for long, but the movie shown for the occasion captured their attention. The visit was so successful that it has grown into a regular service with several films as a major feature and a picture-book story to add the personal touch.

Program planners for organizations are often desperate for materials and will be grateful for a program at the library or films to use at their meeting place. McKinley Park enriched St. Ephraim's afterschool art, music, and social studies clubs by providing films and a live librarian, James Baron, to spark discussions. Recent Brooklyn Public Library policy decisions aimed at greater community involvement have made the regulations covering public use of library facilities more flexible, thus permitting informal or social groups access to meeting rooms. This should draw a wider and more varied group of nonprint-oriented individuals who, in turn, will find movies available for their use.

For those who still feel successful film programs are a matter of luck, here is a project in which I have been involved and which is a valid example of the use of films to reach a community. Crown Heights had changed in a matter of ten years from a reading, middle-class, Catholic and Orthodox Jewish population to a mixture of remaining older residents and less affluent white and black families seeking the older homes left by suburban-bound families. Some of the apartment houses are older walk-ups whose rents attract welfare clients. Although we still had a sound number of consistent library users, the dropping circulation, coupled with an increase in the child population, made it obvious that we were not reaching the newer group. Despite the proximity of a Catholic school whose children passed our door, story hours drew only a maximum of ten children, whereas a few trial film programs ranged up to twenty-five. Under the circumstances it was decided to switch to films as these would appeal to the greatest range of ages and to readers and nonreaders alike.

If Crown Heights had not had a nucleus of familiar children with which to start, another recourse might have been tried as an attraction to the infrequent patron. At New Lots Branch, Marguerite Dodson had access to a psychedelic slide show using two automatic slide projectors, revolving polaroid discs, and impressionistic slides. This was set up in a corner of the public area and either left on during busy hours or turned on when a few interested bodies turned up. None of the studying borrowers objected to the tape of the Beatles' <u>Magical Mystery Tour</u>, and the "cool" successful sight/sound show ran for over a month or until the equipment had to be used for other purposes.

By being in an obvious place at a busy time, the slide show appealed to the reticent or unfamiliar patron who might shy away from events held in a remote meeting room. In this case the event was not tied in with a film series, although it could have been used for advertising such a feature. An automatic cartridge camera in an obvious place can be employed to advertise the types of films shown, or can be used at a branch where the lack of a meeting room makes formal film showings impossible.

At Crown Heights we needed to have those who used the library tell the newcomers about our programs. This would set up a chain reaction—even when the present community had completely shifted, there would still be users who could again repeat the pattern. To start this reaction pattern, we invited every child who came through our door, either alone or on a class visit, to our film program. Window posters reminded those on the way to school.

In order to establish attendance habits it was most important to have the program when the children would be free from homework and family responsibilities. We selected Fridays at 3:30. The programs were held consistently each week even though there was poor attendance at times. The program ran from October through May when good weather, family weekends, and summer commitments made continuation impractical.

As we started our second season, we found we were making inroads. First, we still had most of the previous year's group, now grown to our meeting-room capacity of sixty. Secondly, we were drawing new faces: many having no library cards or cards needing change of address, and some not disposed to taking books out after the show. Most of the children were not accompanied by parents, and their attitudes and behavioral patterns were different from our former patrons. We continued the personal invitations, but now often just as a reminder, and by midseason had to add a second show for children who lived at a distance. Both shows now run at more than capacity—over 120, which is a far cry from the initial 25.

It was not enough just to show the films. It was necessary to personalize the program to make the individual child at ease and the library meaningful for him. During film changes we had group participation. "Counting off" was a game for them and an attendance count for me. If our attendance was low because of bad weather, we gave out crayons and butcher paper and made murals about the film just viewed, then displayed them. This brought friends and parents in to see the drawings.

Since movies are to be an everyday occurrence in all these youngsters' lives, we had brief discussions about film evaluation and film techniques and compared the book to the film version. The favorite movies were stories or cartoons (of a good quality), but occasionally we combined these with other fare. Pantomimes in conjunction with a Marcel Marceau film gave everyone a chance to do his thing. For surprises and special occasions we tried an avant garde simultaneous slide and film feature, sneaked in a story, or drew with magic markers on blank leader like Norman McLaren.

These activities were so well received that they suggested a summer program featuring films interwoven with a variety of arts and crafts, records, and group activities. This drew as many as forty throughout the afternoon, when previously our branch had the usual summer doldrums.

For those who still feel it was a matter of luck and that planning cannot really reach out to the community, let me recount the misadventures of the Film Workshop held at the same branch. This program was designed to give a survey of types of film and then to have the children plan and film their own movies. Despite what I had learned as to timing, advertising, and serving community interests, I did everything wrong, and of course the project failed! Planned when I had the time rather than when it would be best attended, meetings were set for summer mornings. Our children, it developed, were either at summer camp, day camp, or morning public summer school. Concerned that the attendance would be too large for a workable group, the advertising was limited to a library sign, too impersonal and reaching mainly the print-oriented. Finally, only three of the initial casually interested eight came regularly, and even their attendance was broken by family vacations; these children's techniques and plans were, however, most promising. As a final cruncher, the used super-8mm equipment begged from a camera store broke down, and everything came to a grinding halt.

That there is interest in this type of program and that it can be technically successful are indicated by a project produced by Emily Cohen at the Carroll Park Community Library. Using a variety of standard library posters as motifs, she filmed youngsters improvising quick humorous pantomimes on the steps of the library, and the result is a charming little super-8mm film, much like an old-time movie, with its accompanying tape of the Jackson Stomp. It provided the children with an opportunity to participate and with a sense of belonging and immediacy, as they were able to view the film the following week. Intended as a surprise activity for a "Guess What" series, it could be expanded into a drama club or film workshop for film evaluation. Thus the library's film-media service can grow from viewing to doing—much as the print services grew from just borrowing to discussion and writing groups.

Film programs are just one facet of the total picture of communication with the neighborhood. Film programs use some of the techniques found in other services, and other services may include some film usage. But no matter what the service or program, it is basically a case of demand and supply. If your borrowers want new, popular titles, you best serve them by having several copies to meet their demand. If your community has a view of the world which is wider than a traditional book-bound philosophy, then you had better run to catch up with the world's expanding horizons. This is film outreach.

A Changing Library
for a Changing Neighborhood

Marilyn Chandler
Branch Librarian
DeKalb District Library

What happens to a traditional library when it finds itself surrounded by a community whose majority are either semi-literate or too involved in the problems of rats, roaches, hunger, and crumbling tenements to give a damn about the local library? The answer is obvious. If the library maintains its traditional function, it will die a slow, useless death. The DeKalb branch of the Brooklyn Public Library nearly died. Other than serving the few students who dared to venture in with assignments, we were involved only in trying to maintain an appearance of calm, studious activity in the face of roving, aimless teen-agers who had nowhere else to go to get out of the cold, and nothing better to do than to harass the staff, the patrons, and the old, crumbling building. Not interested in books or magazines and finding nothing else available to occupy them, they succeeded in forcing us to close our doors in December of 1968.

We remained closed for a month, during which time several meetings were held to try and find solutions to the severe discipline problems. Every plan the staff volunteered died before it was tried, as each involved money or additional staff, neither of which was forthcoming. We reopened facing the same conditions that had caused our closing except for a stronger force of uniformed guards, and one additional change. The staff had determined that we were not going to allow conditions to degenerate into chaos once again, even if it meant making all the necessary changes ourselves. This is what we have done, and though it is too early to tell for sure, it looks as though

A Changing Library for a Changing Neighborhood 25

DeKalb may not only survive, but may grow into a vital center of the community it is only beginning really to serve.

The beginning of our transformation was small. The staff chipped in to buy a few checker sets, chess sets, cards, dominoes, and other games. Response was immediate, with all the games in use from the time we opened until we closed, and discipline problems dropped sharply, with only isolated incidents and a few heated arguments over the games. Most important, the boys who had formerly caused chaos now spent hours playing games and allowed the staff to help those who came to use the library for study. Late in the spring a phonograph was donated to us. Soul music has been a natural feature of the library ever since.

During the summer months we continued with the games and music, and used the spare time to put the building into the best possible shape, moving collections, weeding, and taking advantage of the new Materials Selection Policy of the Brooklyn Public Library to provide those titles most in demand. Books such as Pimp by Iceberg Slim, and Drum and Mandingo by Kyle Onstott, had previously not met the literary criteria necessary for inclusion in the collection but, under the new policy, met the all-important criteria of public demand and were ordered in large quantities in paperback. Other popular titles were ordered in bulk in paperback editions and displayed in four revolving paperback racks. Newspapers never before available were ordered for the agency: Black Panther, Muhammad Speaks, The Guardian, and others.

The physical plant, a sixty-five-year-old Carnegie building which has never received rehabilitation, was decorated with bright flowered or psychedelic wrapping paper over the bulletin boards, large paper flowers, and other colorful displays to take away from the grimness of falling plaster, dark walls, and general decay. Most important, the summer was spent planning and gathering materials for programs to begin in the fall when school reopened; gaining the full support of the administration of the library for our experiments; and developing new attitudes and new concepts of meaningful library service for our community. Outlined below are some of the programs being put into action now.

To start the season off big, there is a reading contest underway. The child who returns the most books between now and November 8, the last day of Children's Book Week, will win a prize. A book? Hardly. First prize will be a live alligator! Who wants a book? There will be lots of runner-up prizes and a big presentation program on November 8.

We are starting a preschool story hour with a slight twist. While the children are upstairs listening to stories, the mothers will be downstairs having coffee, chatting, and, above all, relaxing. A sewing machine (donated) is available for use any time the library is open, and sewing lessons and instructions for knitting and crocheting, if desired, will be available. There will be recipe-swapping and cooking, and whatever else the mothers would like. A room in the basement, long a catchall, has been cleared and decorated by the staff for use by the women in the area.

The auditorium at DeKalb, a large sterile room, is being turned over to the teen-agers for a few hours each week for use as a clubroom. The kids will be responsible for fixing up a corner the way they want it from a pile of lamps, tables, and sturdy fireproof furniture (donated). They will set up their own house rules and will police themselves to a large degree, with staff members looking in only occasionally to make certain that some degree of order is maintained. They will be allowed the use of the room for as long as they follow their own rules, having a place where they can play cards, dance, or just talk to one another without being hushed every time they raise their voices to a normal pitch or utter a few harmless profanities. We grant that this plan is a calculated risk, but it is one we all feel is well worth taking, and if it fails, so what? At least we will have tried something.

Other programs underway or being planned include both the orthodox and the experimental. We will be having as many class visits as we can handle, weekly story hours, weekly film programs for children, read-aloud programs on Saturdays (a children's librarian is not necessary for this type of story hour), a checkers and chess tournament consisting of our regular players, a contest with a prize for the person rounding up the greatest number of overdue books and returning them, an arts and crafts program including a "paint-in," mask making from papier-mâché, decorating for Christmas, a remedial reading program, a theater workshop with professionals (volunteer) working with all age groups, and whatever else we can think up. We are also working on plans for a young adult film series, classes in photography (if we can get the needed equipment), and several other ideas still in the thinking stage.

Perhaps the most significant change of all has been in the attitudes of the staff. It is far easier to hide behind rules and regulations than it is to consider the community and its members as the most important thing at all times. Charging fines for overdue books and taking away the library cards of those who were unable to pay was a problem for us for a long time. This was solved unwittingly by our delinquent boys, who stole our money so often we were finally able to convince the administration that we should discontinue charging fines and get rid of all the money in the agency. This has not only removed a serious temptation but, more important, has resulted in the restoration of cards for many and the removal of a tremendous barrier between the library and its users. With the removal of money problems, the clerical staff has been able to establish a much friendlier relationship with the borrowers, and a change in the general atmosphere is apparent. Now that the area does not have to be guarded against possible theft, neighborhood boys who have long been fascinated by the action of the photocharger can see its full operation and even operate it themselves. Two have become so adept at its operation that they can take over during the very busy afternoon hours. They enjoy doing it, it eases the load on the clerks, and they are beginning to feel that they have some part in the library. Other boys are busy painting bulletin boards, fixing up furniture for the clubroom, talking about other programs they would like to see in the library, and generally getting involved with the operations going on. The advantages of this should be evident.

Our prime concern now is to make people feel as welcome as possible and to make certain they receive whatever information they come to get. If rules must be relaxed in order for this to happen, they are relaxed. No one is forced to leave without the material he needs because he lacks the necessary identification for a library card. It is far more important to make certain he has the desired material with a minimum of red tape and confusion. For many, it is a first visit to a library, and that first impression must be a good one if they are to return.

Anticipating a number of questions and criticism concerning our new philosophy of service, we shall attempt to answer some already presented to us by other staff members in the Brooklyn system:

1. <u>Have the programs solved all the problems which existed before they were put into effect?</u>

Of course not. Discipline problems have diminished to the point where we have not had a serious outbreak for seven months. The problem of theft remains a serious one. None of our original games is left, our first phonograph was stolen, and we are subjected to frequent burglaries despite the installation of an expensive burglar alarm. We replace the games as they are taken, a second phonograph has been donated to us and is in use, and the burglary situation will improve only when a solution to the narcotics problem is found. All we can do is to secure our equipment to the best of our ability and hope the alarm will discourage thieves. Being human, we naturally become discouraged, but all we have to do is think back to how the situation used to be, and we are ready to keep trying.

2. *Does music have a place in a library? Doesn't it serve only to distract serious students?*

The noise level in the library has decreased noticeably since music was introduced. Most students today seem to study by radio or television sets and are accustomed to music. We have had very few complaints (three in six months), and these were not from regular users of the library. The young people have control over what is played and often bring in their own 45's. Other than a little finger popping and some singing along with the record, which is fine with us, the sound is not distracting. The phonograph is located in the children's room along with the games, and though the sound carries over to the adult side, study is possible. There are few real research students using the branch, and those who do come in, do so during the quieter morning hours, not after school.

3. *Where can one get equipment such as sewing machines, furniture, phonographs, and the like?*

All our equipment and many supplies for our arts and crafts programs have come from volunteers who believe in what we are trying to do. All it really takes is a phone call to someone with a basement or an attic, children who have outgrown toys, and so on. We do not expect new or expensive equipment and are not afraid to ask friends, businessmen, or strangers to help us find what we need. Once started, we often have more offers than we need and, indeed, have had to turn down some television sets, washing machines, and doll carriages (but found use for a live alligator)!

4. *All these programs are fine for a community center, but what do they have to do with a library? Aren't you forgetting the purpose of a library, and the use of books and reading?*

Good question, and it has been asked many times in different ways. Think about it. Most libraries in poverty areas are suffering from losses in circulation and underutilization. Most members of the community are unaware of the services available and feel that libraries are all right for their children or

A Changing Library for a Changing Neighborhood

scholars, but have nothing to offer them. The only way to let people know what can be found inside is to get them in, and the only way to do that is to offer them something they want badly enough to come in and get. Right now, in our area, books are not that important. A sewing machine available to a mother of several children with no machine for mending might well be. Offering preschool mothers a cup of coffee is a means of getting them together inside the library. Over the coffee we can then begin to determine what they would like from the library. This could lead to programs on health, child care, consumer education, or whatever topics they might be interested in, as well as introducing to them the fact that we have material on sewing, cooking, or dealing with the landlord as well as scholarly works. At least, they will be exposed to the full scale of information and services provided by their public library and will be encouraged to use them fully.

The potential for the teen-agers is just as great, if not more so. After the clubroom becomes an established thing, a series of programs they want to see or hear can be made possible, whether it be a film or speaker on narcotics, a karate demonstration, someone to help them find jobs, or something in which we would never imagine they might be interested. The possibilities are infinite.

We on the DeKalb staff are, first and last, librarians and have never lost sight of our true goals—the performance of excellent librarianship. The means we use might differ from the traditional, but the traditional means failed us some time ago. We have found that we cannot serve our community to the fullest by using the tried and true methods of the past, and so we are trying new methods. In the absence of any type of community center in this rather desolate area, we have perhaps taken on some of the functions of a center, but what better way to utilize a library than to open it to the community? When we take to the streets with posters, drums, and banners, or give away live alligators, we are only selling our services by letting people know that the library isn't just a book center for scholars, but a fun place for anyone to visit, with something to offer almost any group.

The entire staff at DeKalb is working harder than we have ever worked before, but with a difference. We are all ready to admit that we are having fun, the kids are having a ball, life at DeKalb isn't the dreary existence it used to be, and, quite incidentally, it has been quite some time since we have had to tell a rowdy teen-ager to keep quiet and received as a reply, "Fuck you, this place ain't no good nohow!"

The Coney Island Community: A Case Study

Martin Lubin, formerly Branch Librarian
Coney Island Branch Library

Now District Librarian
Prospect District Library

New York is probably the most heterogeneous city in the world. The Borough of Brooklyn itself is a complex social, political, economic, cultural, and ethnic community of more than two and one-half million residents. Coney Island is world-famous for its boardwalk and amusement area; however, a block away from the deteriorating stands and crowded beach is a virtual city in miniature. This is the real Coney Island of the well-to-do and the poor; the black and the white; of Puerto Ricans, Italians, and Jews; of slums, high-rise cooperative apartment houses, and even a private, fenced-off residential area protected by its own police force. It is a community of diverse, often antagonistic, interests where one can find virtually every possible shade of opinion.

Coney Island, then, is a microcosm, a diminutive example in which one can identify all the forces at work in society. It is also an area in which the library has had a unique opportunity to establish meaningful relationships with a wide range of groups within the community. Equally important is the fact that in establishing new relationships the library has been able to maintain one of its most important traditional virtues; it has remained open and available to all sides of a controversy in an area often racked by dissension. The library has often been described as neutral territory, where all parties can come and meet together without appearing to give ground and lose prestige. The community, and particularly local leaders, have come to hold the library and the librarian in considerable esteem. An additional factor of great importance is the fact that the library is housed in a relatively new, attractive building with a large auditorium and comfortable air conditioning, and located at the very center of the Coney Island area. These factors, combined with the desire of the staff to become active participants in the community they serve and to initiate contacts with other agencies and organizations, have made the library a focus for community activity.

Traditionally libraries have worked with various organizations in the community. Schools and social clubs have often made use of library services as adjuncts to their programs. The library was generally seen as a supplement providing diversion and entertainment rather than as an agency of basic importance and usefulness. The degree of involvement by library staff in these organizations was nil, although much effort was often expended in preparing book talks and class visits.

A change in the attitude and goals on the part of the professional librarian and the consumer of library services has resulted in marked departures from old norms. First, the number and kinds of groups demanding and receiving library service have been increasing rapidly. Second, the librarian has taken the initiative to make the library felt as a vital force in the community. In the Coney Island area this has been achieved largely as a result of increased cooperation with other service agencies and community organizations. In effect, the library has become a partner in a broad program of change.

The following list shows the wide range as well as the number of groups with which the Coney Island Branch Library works:

<u>Community development organizations</u>
 Coney Island Chamber of Commerce
 Coney Island Community Corporation
 Coney Island Community Council
 Professional Services Advisory Committee

<u>Educational agencies</u>
 New York City Board of Education: District 21
 New York City Board of Education: Bureau for the
  Education of the Physically Handicapped
 Operation Head Start
 Our Lady of Solace R.C. School
 Yeshiva Sharai Zadek

<u>Municipal agencies</u>
 Coney Island Houses

The Coney Island Community: A Case Study

<u>Municipal agencies</u> (continued)
    Gravesend Houses
    Haber Houses
    Mayor's Urban Task Force
    New York City Housing Authority
    New York City Police Dept., 60th Precinct

<u>Religious institutions</u>
    Congregation Sharai Zadek
    Naomi A.M.E. Zion Church
    Our Lady of Solace R.C. Church
    Thirty-first Street Talmud Torah

<u>Social and cultural agencies</u>
    Haber Houses Senior Citizens
    Hadassah of Seagate
    Luna Park Women's Club
    Luna Park Toddler Land
    Seagate Senior Citizens

<u>Social service agencies</u>
    Brooklyn Hebrew Home and Hospital for the Aged
    Coney Island Child Care Center
    Coney Island Community Family Center
    Coney Island Hospital
    Coney Island Mental Health Services of the Jewish
        Board of Guardians
    Hirschman YM-YWHA
    Phoenix House
    Youth Board

Library involvement has ranged from providing meeting space for such important groups as the Mayor's Urban Task Force to extensive programming for educational and social service agencies. Between these extremes is a wide range of areas of participation and cooperation. Relationships which begin when the library makes its meeting room available to a group often evolve toward active cooperative planning as the new group becomes at home in the library and a rapport is developed with the staff. By having staff members attend community meetings and participate as actively as possible, an awareness of the library's program is brought to a much larger and diversified public than would otherwise be possible. In addition, the librarian becomes exposed to the needs of the community in a very direct manner. The result of this approach in the Coney Island area has been the establishment of wide-ranging programs that have brought real life to the library.

Here are some concrete examples of the kinds of programs which have successfully been put into practice in Coney Island. It would be impossible to detail every program with which the library has been associated, and many unique and interesting efforts have been omitted in order to concentrate on those having the widest possible applicability.

The Professional Services Advisory Council of Coney Island, or PSAC, is an organization whose membership includes representatives of public and private nonprofit, service-giving agencies operating in the Coney Island community. Its purpose is to plan and promote improved facilities and services for the area's residents. PSAC is an impressive example of growing cooperation on the part of individual professional workers and service agencies at the local level.

The PSAC serves as a forum where all problems affecting the Coney Island area can be discussed rationally in an atmosphere of mutual respect and professional objectivity. The organization has gained respect and recognition for its role as mediator in disputes threatening to divide the community. Topics that often come up for discussion by the group include housing, education, and welfare services. After evaluation of the situation, the PSAC often issues position papers. This was the case in a recent controversy over the composition of the Coney Island Hospital's Community Advisory Board. It is indicative of the prestige of the PSAC that the current head of the Community Advisory Board and the hospital administrator twice met with representatives of the organization at the hospital in order to present their views.

Members of the professional staff of the library have taken an active role in the PSAC, and the majority of the group's meetings are held in the library. The result has been a new image for the library. The librarian has been able to take an active part in planning a wide range of events, activities, and services of which in the past he might at best have been only vaguely aware. The library has become an equal among the agencies providing professional services to the area, and in many instances the ability of its representatives has given it an active leadership role. Members of the library's professional staff are sought out to assist at planning meetings held at other agencies. Requests for the use of facilities and services now come from agency heads who in the past were either unaware of or ignored the possibility of working with the library. The library staff, in turn, has been made more alert to the needs of groups that have underutilized the library because they feel its services are not geared to meeting their needs.

The result has been the establishment of programs and services for the Youth Board, Phoenix House (a narcotics rehabilitation center), and the Board of Education at the District level; a number of programs sponsored by the Department of Social Services or established through antipoverty funds; and many others. The mutual assistance offered by various agencies has drawn them together in an effort to provide better overall service to the community.

Students are the largest single group of library users, and their needs have been the subject of a good deal of soul-searching on the part of school and library officials. Considerable effort has been made to identify and define the areas of responsibility of the school and of the public library. To evaluate this complex problem and really to resolve it, a working relationship between the library administration and the education establishment is necessary. This has proved extremely difficult.

At the branch level the usual approach is to contact each school in the area and build the best possible relationship with the school administrators and the school librarian. The result is often a series of class visits to the library for elementary and junior high school students. The degree of cooperation beyond this limited but extremely useful and highly successful type of programming depends upon the initiative of the librarian and the receptivity of school personnel.

Through contacts made at meetings of the PSAC, a series of meetings were arranged between the branch librarian and the district superintendent of schools and their staffs. A wide range of issues was discussed in an effort to come to grips with those problems that might be resolved on the local level. The result has been a uniformly high level of cooperation with all the schools in the area.

The general atmosphere of cooperation that has been established with the schools on both a personal and a district-wide level has stimulated the development of new programs aimed at educators as well as at students. One program of unusual interest provides for a series of return visits to the library for students attending the area's experimental More Effective School. The aim of the return visits is to establish the library habit through monthly visits following the original class-visit program. Another program was developed to provide educational assistants—paraprofessionals working in the schools—with basic library and storytelling skills. Both programs have been extremely successful and rewarding for librarians, teachers, and students and may serve as an example of the many innovative programs that can be undertaken on the basis of cooperation between the library and the schools in a community.

Probably no organization is more interested in and responsive to library services in the Coney Island area than Phoenix House. At first glance a narcotics rehabilitation center might look like a rather unlikely source of patronage for the public library, but the reverse has proved to be true. All the residents of Phoenix House from the director down are former addicts. Running the center is a cooperative effort; all the residents pool their money, and each is assigned a specific job. What the visitor finds at Phoenix House is not a chamber of horrors, but an ordered community filled with warmth, excitement, and hope.

When Phoenix House began operations in Coney Island, members of the library staff were among the first to visit and welcome the newcomers. One can imagine that this was not the reception generally offered by wary neighbors. The result has been a steady and close association between the House and the library. A point is made to have new staff members visit and tour the center where they are introduced to each of the residents. New arrivals at Phoenix House are soon introduced to the library, where they are given a tour of the building and the opportunity to fill out library cards. Many return frequently to obtain books in the areas of psychology, philosophy, and religion.

The Education Department at Phoenix House has asked the library to provide programs and, in turn, has provided speakers for library-sponsored programs dealing with narcotics addiction. Speakers from the branch have given brief talks at Phoenix House, and a series of film showings at the library have been attended enthusiastically by groups from the center. One cannot help feeling elated by the success of this type of cooperative effort.

Mention teen-agers to an adult, and you are apt to get a strange look or shrug of the shoulders as a reply. Adolescents are generally held to be a noisy, nasty, disruptive group whose constant hell-raising drives adults into a frenzy. Still, teen-agers are a sizable portion of the library's public and include all the potential adult library users as well. The question is how does the librarian determine the needs of this group, meet those needs, and maintain a minimum of sanity in the process?

The need to act frequently as a disciplinarian is one of the most difficult and disturbing aspects of working with teen-agers. While matters can occasionally get out of hand to the extent that it is necessary to call the police for assistance, this can only be regarded as an immediate expedient for short-term relief rather than as a solution to the problem. The crux of the difficulty is the problem of relating library service to this age group. In an effort to work toward such a goal in the Coney Island area, the library has established and maintained an important and reciprocally useful relationship with the Youth Board.

The Youth Board has worked to organize the youth of the area in order to provide them with a sense of identity and belonging, to give them experience in running their own affairs, to provide a mechanism by which they can have a voice in community affairs, and to utilize whatever opportunities for education and employment that might be available. After the organization of formal groups complete with bylaws and elected officials, the next step was to find a meeting place. Since the Youth Board had worked with the library staff on several other occasions, a request for weekly use of a meeting room in the library was made and approved. Further cooperation has been encouraged by having library staff participate in the planning of a dance sponsored by the group. The group's leaders and the library staff have begun to explore further possibilities for cooperative programming. The relationship which has been established is an example of how the library can work with other service agencies to reach special groups within the community.

The library's work with local organizations in the Coney Island area can be divided into two categories. The first consists of local women's clubs, groups of senior citizens, and others who seek traditional library programs, such as book talks, which are requested and provided as frequently as possible. This service is given since it is the library's policy that all members of the community should receive the kind of library service they need and want. It is also the library's policy that not only should service be provided regularly to local library users but efforts should be made to extend facilities to those who are not currently consumers of library services.

The library attempts to reach this second group by working with local independent organizations. Many of these agencies have boards of directors made up of community leaders and are funded in the main through antipoverty appropriations. These organizations represent people who either do not use or underutilize the library's resources.

Many of the local antipoverty groups in Coney Island have been contacted by the library. Some, becoming aware of the services the library had provided for other groups, have taken the initiative in exploring possible areas of cooperation. One drawback has been that there are many agencies operating in the Coney Island area, some with similar programs and frequently competing for funds. Although some groups have become established and powerful, many have proved to be relatively short-term experiments. In all it is a very difficult situation in which to make long-range plans. Instead, programs have been provided on an individual basis, and have usually lasted only as long as the agency functioned or the leader who had participated in planning remained in the community. The library has worked with such organizations as the Coney Island Family Center, the Puerto Rican Federation, and a number of Head Start groups. The programs have ranged from trips to the library to obtain cards and be taken on a tour, to consumer education and vocational guidance for adults and story hours for preschool children.

An area just being explored by the library in Coney Island is working with civic and fraternal groups within the black and Puerto Rican communities. One such local fraternal group is called the Seven Wise Men. This group takes an active part in community activities, and contact was first made with it at the planning session for the dance sponsored by the Youth Board mentioned above. The result was a meeting with representatives of the organization at the library, and the scheduling of two programs for children attending a store-front community center sponsored by the Seven Wise Men. While efforts to work with community organizations in Coney Island still fall short of the goal of reaching everyone in the community, the steps which have been taken have achieved significant results.

Ask the People—
They Know Where It Is

Addie Powell
Specialist in Work with Adults
Williamsburgh District Library

Getting people to use the library often depends on getting to know the people. Williamsburgh District has tried to solve its problem of lack of library use by going directly to the community for answers. Where it is, simply, is where the people are. The five library communities in Williamsburgh District offer interesting and arresting patterns of cultural diversity: Hasidic Jews, Spanish-speaking Americans, black Americans, Italians, and Polish Americans, each gathered together in independent communities.

Knowing where the people are suggested keys to methods for effective communication, design in programming, and suitable publicity. Whatever differences there may be among cultures, sooner or later all human beings are concerned with what will help them eat, sleep, work, and play. In reaching out to meet these universal human needs within the diverse communities, programs at Williamsburgh District have followed the patterns of mores within the cultures themselves.

Where people live, how they live, what they eat, how they play, who are their heroes and leaders, and, most important, how can the library help enhance their daily life are questions which can be answered by simple, careful observation. Go to the well and drink; ask the people—they know where it is.

One of the most successful programs at Williamsburgh was in food preparation. "Everybody ought to eat the same thing. Most people do eat the same thing. But everybody's got a different way to fix it." This is a good summary made by a regular participant in the programs. The series was cosponsored by the Fort Greene Department of Health and Nutrition, Cumberland Hospital, the Consumers Buying Club, the Department of Social Services, and Brooklyn Public Library.

Designed to help consumers purchase, prepare, and plan more wholesome meals for the family, with an emphasis on condiments favored among minority cultures, the series included illustrated lectures on foods basic to good health; how to budget, market, and detect unfair selling practices; how to organize buying clubs; and a final session on Puerto Rican and soul-food cookery.

Enthusiasm and interest were sparked at each session by a brief fifteen-minute "Taste-in," usually of two dishes prepared from surplus foods from the Department of Social Services. Donated foods are very unpopular among welfare recipients and are often left unused or given away; the demonstrations showed how the foods could be fixed to please the tastes of local residents. With an average attendance of twenty at each meeting, discussion was lively, and book circulation, especially of paperback cookbooks, very good.

The most effective leadership in both planning and presentation of these programs came from the Health Aides, women from the community, most of them welfare recipients; they knew what the community wanted. It was their idea to emphasize favored condiments, ethnic cookery, and uses for donated foods. Although five hundred leaflets prepared by Health Aides were distributed, the largest audience was drawn by Aides and a librarian strolling through a nearby housing project and telling people about the meeting just prior to the program.

Programs were presented alternately at the Consumers Buying Club and at the community library; those at the Buying Club were better attended than those in the library, although one would have thought the facilities less comfortable: exhaust fans blowing full blast, orange crates and broken folding chairs for seating, and Italian ices on sale at the entrance.

During a special meeting to evaluate the series, a Health Aide offered reasons for this preference: "The general feeling about libraries is in connection with education; education to many of the people for whom the programs were designed was seldom a happy experience. Residents seldom used the library after they had finished formal schooling. To attend a meeting in the library meant a change in dress; to attend meetings at the Buying Club one could drop by from shopping dressed as one was without changing." This tells us a good deal about the degree of informality that may be desirable at a community library if it wishes to attract users. One Puerto Rican woman followed through with seven groups, reaching approximately 217 additional women with similar programs modeled on the library series and presented in Spanish.

Like food, lodging is a fundamental interest in the Fort Greene community. To respond to this interest Walt Whitman Library, in cooperation with the Brooklyn Board of Realtors, presented four programs. Circumstances were difficult. The series was held in the middle of the winter, and heavy snows kept down attendance at the first two meetings; the last two were better attended, but, in both cases, the speaker was not able to appear. Fortunately the women who came to the speakerless meetings were well informed, articulate, and able to carry on a successful discussion without a leader.

Among the reasons for the near failure of the series were the reluctance of Board of Realtor speakers to travel through Brooklyn ghettos at night and the fact that the librarian had not estimated correctly the caliber of the potential audience. It was expected that there would be more men in the audience than women, that tenants and landlord problems would dominate the discussion, and that the audience would not be so experienced or well informed as it proved to be. No one expected the overwhelming and persistent interest in acquiring title, buying property, and renovating brownstone houses.

The leaders did not seem to mind small audiences, and the audiences did not let the breakdown in plans deter them from pursuing the interest for which they came. The atmosphere was very congenial and pleasant. The women were responsive, brought questions, shared experiences with the leaders and among themselves, and even told the librarian how to do better with this kind of program next time.

Enhancing the group's self-image is very important among minorities; there is always an audience very ready to respond to any effort in this direction. Opportunities to celebrate significant ethnic events or honor special heroes is given priority in attention at Williamsburgh. Book talks to Jewish women's groups which immortalize their heroines—and history is well stocked with them—not only spark interest in Jewish women, but can open avenues to further reading about women leaders from other ethnic groups. Book talks with Golda Meir as a central focus of interest are very popular and afford opportunity to introduce women heroes such as Indira Gandhi from India.

Like ethnic minorities, women find special appeal in anything that will enhance their vanity or personal self-image. Talking with women in communities and brushing across them in Brooklyn shopping centers, we noticed that familiar faces from library communities were found browsing through dress-pattern catalogs in department stores more often than in the library.

So Williamsburgh began a unique service for its women and subscribed to monthly counter-size dress-pattern catalogs: Simplicity, McCall's, Butterick, and Vogue. The women can now browse through the latest modes in a leisurely way, combine their own ideas with those in one or more patterns, and copy the order number to order directly or drop by their favorite sewing department and purchase. Shopping time is cut considerably and, of course, while in the library women are likely to pick up a book on sewing and perhaps a best seller, just in case there is enough time left to read it. Current issues of the pattern books, displayed on dictionary or atlas stands, are for reference use; back issues circulate when seasonal popularity is over.

Like food, an interest in clothes and fashions has a way of bringing women together as few other mutual interests can. Women who never knew each other before have met in the use of this service, and, when they do, there is much talk. In one community library a Spanish-American and a black American woman chanced to meet in search of new fashions, and before the afternoon was over the two had designed a unique creation combining the Spanish mode with popular African garb.

There is no one way or only way to follow when working with people; many approaches have merit. We have to find one that works for us where we are in getting done what the community needs done. One thing you can count on. The people know where it's at. Ask them, watch them, respond to them, help them, and your library will become the busy place you want it to be.

The Community Coordinator Program

Thelma Black
Community Coordinator

When a community coordinator looks at the area in which he will be working, he observes run-down or abandoned houses, broken glass, and garbage-filled streets. He finds that the proportion of persons receiving welfare is several times higher than that of the city as a whole, health records are poorer, and crime rates are higher. He may well wonder how far one can get taking books outside the walls of the library to people living in these circumstances.

When the community coordinator project began seven years ago, antipoverty programs had not been established, and those who lived in deprived areas were largely unorganized except for their churches. The coordinators' first problem was how to find persons with whom to work. People are suspicious of do-gooders offering free services. Our first job was to gain confidence. We had to become a part of the community in order to prove our skill and our interest. We joined groups and worked actively with them so that we could understand their points of view and relate our materials to them in a meaningful way.

Our job is to create awareness of library services and resources, prove that our materials are relevant, generate an atmosphere of library acceptance, and promote library usage. As the liaison between the library and the community, we add "in the right place" to "the right book for the right person."

Library files in Brooklyn have turned up reports and pictures of community activities back to the turn of the century. The big difference now is that some librarians have been freed completely from branch schedules and responsibilities so that they may be available to present library materials wherever and whenever they are needed.

Community coordinators must have an infectious enthusiasm for the library and what it can do, a sincere interest in people, and devotion to a job that defies calendars and clocks. Plans and activities must remain flexible so that they may be modified to satisfy the practical demands of the moment. Because word spreads rapidly of one's willingness to listen and to help and because helpers are often difficult to find, coordinators find themselves cast in many roles: neighbor, counselor, social worker, and teacher as well as librarian.

Sometimes the solution to a problem is simple, as when a girl who had been looking for a job was sent to see me, and I referred her to the State Employment Office. She reported to work the following day. Small was our service in time or energy, but her family was convinced that the library was the greatest. Cases such as this point up the need for one of the library's images to be that of an information center.

Though people move out of their established routine reluctantly, most are at least somewhat motivated by a desire for self-improvement and for a better self-image, or by their concern for their children. Residents in one area requested assistance in forming a block association. Not only did we work with them on initial plans, but we also supplied them with books and pamphlets on how to run a club and related subjects. After a chaotic session, the film Speech: Conducting a Meeting was presented as the main feature of their next gathering.

A group of mothers of preschool children came to my office one day to discuss difficulties they were having in understanding their four- and five-year-olds. Among other things the children had been unwilling to participate in activities from which the parents were excluded. This developed into an informal evening in the home of one of the mothers where the films Frustrating Fours and Fascinating Fives and The Pleasure Is Mutual were presented and discussed.

These early contacts took place before the war on poverty was initiated. Its agencies are now reaching deeper and deeper into the disadvantaged communities, spreading hope and creating an appreciation of and hunger for education as the key to making this hope a reality. Our task is now not quite so difficult as it was.

In areas filled with antipoverty programs and mothers supported by Aid to Dependent Children who are required and paid to attend classes, it is relatively easy to contact hundreds of persons who would otherwise be very difficult to locate. We find that individuals in charge of antipoverty and adult education projects are easily persuaded to include the library in their programs. Such involvement often includes work with in-service training units, book lists and discussions, manned exhibits, film programs, career clinics, articles for community newspapers, preschool programs, assistance in establishing community centers, setting up of book deposits, and assistance in the selection of titles to be purchased for nonlibrary agencies with money provided through grants.

Although we work with all age groups, we concentrate on adults primarily. Since children and adolescents are made aware of library services through regularly scheduled story hours, film programs, class visits, and school assignments, we forward most requests for service for young people to the various library units.

Organized adult groups generally fall into one of four categories: civic, parent, adult education, or senior citizens. We work with all of them, cooperating with them in such a way that they will develop successful programs and recognize the value of library resources in their development. We stress the value of the library as a practical source of information and a useful tool.

Everyone likes films. In an area where many people are not accustomed to reading, more is often accomplished with a good film followed by a lively discussion than through the circulation of books. Sometimes borrowed books are not read; sometimes those that are read are misunderstood. Even films may be misinterpreted. Discussion offers an opportunity to correct misinterpretation, but stimulating a lively discussion after a film presentation is not always an easy task. Although groups are more articulate now than they were four or five years ago, a film, followed by a coffee break during which small groups form voluntarily, often stimulates more lively discussions than do the more formal approaches.

All our programs include library orientation and an opportunity to register and to borrow books. We try to schedule at least two meetings with each group. The first is often held in their regular meeting place. The second visit, usually in the library, varies according to their educational experience and language proficiency. In the case of Spanish-speaking groups the return visit consists of a few minutes pointing out the location of the collections on Puerto Rican culture, basic education, and foreign languages, followed by a film of Puerto Rican culture and an opportunity to return books, browse, and borrow additional materials. Newcomers are registered, and members of the original group pick up their library cards. With other groups we may include such information as where to find and how to use general reference books and the card catalog.

We work with a number of organizations dedicated to broadening the knowledge and interest of youths and challenging them intellectually. Three types with which I have worked are tutorial programs; college and career clubs, established to inspire youngsters with an enthusiasm for higher or specialized education and knowledge of ways and means of attaining it; and S.A.V.E., a tutorial program designed by the Longshoreman's Association in cooperation with several institutions of higher learning in New York City to prepare high school graduates who are holders of the general certificate to meet minimum standards for admission to community colleges or schools for technical training.

The coordinators work with established institutions of the community as well as with organizations. For example, the Department of Health places a Nutrition Bus on the street during National Nutrition Week, and we always go along to register borrowers for the library and to circulate materials on nutrition and dieting.

We cooperate with schools in various ways, such as establishing in library agencies Education Shelves where current materials that we feel will be of professional interest to employees of the Board of Education and other school personnel are placed; judging various school contests; and playing an active role in spring workshops for parents of children who will be entering school for the first time in the fall. We participated in the kickoff of a Principals Book Club in one school, cooperated to keep it alive during the summer, and had certificates from the library to present as awards to its participants. We are a part of Career Day activities, not only representing the library profession, but also displaying photographs of employees in nonprofessional titles, presenting vocationally oriented films, and displaying a selection of materials on a variety of non-library-connected jobs.

There are many individuals who are not connected with organizations or institutions; there are also members of organizations who need assistance on personal matters. Recognizing these facts, we have done several things to help those who come seeking our services and to locate those who do not.

One community coordinator went from door to door in a local low-cost housing project in an effort to inform its residents of the library's resources and services. My approach is different. Through an agreement with the manager of a housing

The Community Coordinator Program   47

project, I receive a monthly list of new residents and send letters from the library welcoming them to their new homes. Each letter asks for an opportunity to visit and discuss the library. When invited, I go to see the potential library patron. I also knock on the doors of a sampling of those who do not respond to the letter, tell them who I am, present my card, and hope to be admitted. These visits were made especially preceding the advent of special programs likely to be of interest to new people in the neighborhood.

While visiting individuals is an admirable way to introduce library services to nonusers, it is impossible to meet a significant number of people not affiliated with organized groups in this manner. We had to devise some way to reach large numbers of people in a relatively short time. An auto van was our answer. We call our van program "Sidewalk Service."

The van is specially equipped with an auxiliary generator to provide power for floodlights, loudspeakers, and a tape recorder. It also carries racks on which books are displayed, a table, and two chairs. At first we brought along a typewriter for registration, but discovered that typing the cards on the spot was not feasible, so we developed a form from which cards are typed after we have returned to the office. The van makes stops at street corners, parks, housing projects, community happenings, and any other place where people gather or pass in the normal course of the day's activities.

We arrive at a stop, set up for business, and turn on the tape which plays music and messages about the library and its services. The tape is punctuated regularly by the song you've no doubt heard on radio and television, "It's the latest, it's the greatest, it's the li-bi-ree." Often there's a chorus joining in by the end of the song. Each coordinator is scheduled to use the van on the streets of his district one day a week. He may also use it in connection with a special program, such as a community function or for showing outdoor movies.

Unlike our bookmobiles, the van visits areas near library branches that are underutilized. All materials borrowed from the van must be returned to a regular library agency. Also, unlike the bookmobiles, van stops are not published, and many locales are visited only once. Two basic points that we try to make are that library services are free and that we have something for everyone. People are amazed that they can register on the spot and take books home with them.

For many people Sidewalk Service is their first real contact with the library. Learning of its facilities in such an informal way makes them aware that librarians are approachable and interested in helping. New users are touched by the idea that the library cared enough to send materials out to them, and it does the heart good when one is able to fill a request made by a skeptic who asks for something that he feels is outlandish and impossible.

In most places the van is an instantaneous hit, especially with the children. When we park, they often spring up as if by magic even before we have had time to set up our displays. Frequently we take a storyteller along; the children are delighted, and sometimes we even see an adult standing close by and listening. Brochures in English, Spanish, or Italian are given to passersby. We display a variety of books, including an abundant supply of paperbacks, and we stress services as well as materials.

Adults are usually more skeptical and reserved than children. There are those who simply say "Not interested" as they pass. Sometimes, however, they pass again and again, and one can persuade them at least to listen and perhaps to join and borrow books. Not always, though. Once, there was a man who seemed curious though distant. When the opportunity presented itself for us to talk, he declared that he could not read because he worked all the time. I responded with, "Surely you don't work twenty-four hours a day." To which he replied, "Yes, ma'am, I do, and sometimes more." I had to admit to myself that you can't win them all and gave up.

The initial procedure in borrowing a book from the van involves presenting identification, signing for a card, and having a date-due card placed in the book pocket or a paperback stamped with the date due. The registrar explains to the new cardholder where the branch most convenient for him is located and that he will be expected to pick up his card there. He is also told that all library materials borrowed may be returned to any agency of the system. Many adults registered in this manner are oblivious to the libraries in their communities and have to be shown their locations on a map. Most of these new borrowers do find their local branches, return the books, and pick up their cards.

The manager of one of our community libraries reports, "It is very gratifying to see the number of adults as well as children who come in for library cards that they have applied for on the van. Many of the new borrowers have a look of having discovered something new and wonderful."

Of course, some of our successes are fortuitous rather than planned, as in the case of a high school senior who came to the community coordinator's office for advice. He was interested in attending college but had no funds. The coordinator, having heard that a recruiter from one of the small colleges was in town, arranged for a meeting between the two, and the youth is now in college on a working scholarship.

Another of the community coordinator functions is to be ever sensitive to the desires and needs of the community. In one case this resulted in the development of what we call a Puerto Rican Culture Collection. The project began when representatives from the Puerto Rican Culture Program, a federally funded group, expressed concern over the scarcity of such materials in the library. They were especially desirous of having materials available in Spanish. The collection encompasses Puerto Rican art, travel, history, biography, and literature and includes prints by outstanding Puerto Rican artists and recordings of music and poetry.

The library placed attractive posters throughout the community announcing the existence of the collection and inviting the public to visit the library during its opening week. Staff of the Puerto Rican Culture Program worked with us in developing the project and furnished Puerto Rican art objects, paintings, and mimeographed sheets of information about Puerto Rico in Spanish and English. Representatives of the organization also served as hostesses in the library throughout the week. They greeted those who visited, explained the art objects, and discussed Puerto Rico. Members of groups and individual visitors were allowed to try their hand with some of the musical instruments.

We soon learned, however, that this collection was not sufficient to meet the practical needs of the Puerto Ricans in our community. It was then expanded to include English-Spanish dictionaries and language records; English classics for the benefit of students who have recently moved to the mainland; practical titles on auto, radio, and television repairing; fundamentals of electronics and child care; and cookbooks and books on flower arrangement. Also added to the collection were books of United States history and travel, adventure, science, hobbies, and popular novels on a variety of reading levels. Books to be read to preschoolers are also included. The entire collection is in Spanish. Other interests of the community were met through the development of an Afro-American History Collection and the presentation of an Afro-American fashion show.

Special programs and projects may induce individuals to visit the library, but the new patrons will become users only if they find a concerned and interested staff when they arrive. All agencies must be participants in any effort to encourage nonusers to become users of the library. The cooperation of clerks as well as of librarians is basic to the success of the effort. There is also a tremendous advantage in having someone on all agency staffs who can communicate with each resident of the community in his native tongue. Not only will the library be sure that the borrower understands the information we are imparting, but it will also establish a rapport that may not otherwise be obtainable.

Although it is difficult to measure exactly the results of projects such as ours, it is evident that we are making a contribution to the community. An ever increasing number of persons is contacting us for reference assistance, and persons who began using the library under the direction of and with dependence upon the community coordinator are now becoming independent users of our collections. Others who have been patrons of branches, but somewhat in awe of the main building, have been introduced to special services there and been convinced that they can receive the same individualized attention in the larger building as in their local agencies.

Being a library community coordinator is an often exhausting, sometimes frustrating, but almost always satisfying position. Making the library a vital part of community life even in the most educationally advanced neighborhoods is no easy task. It should not seem strange, then, that progress may at first be slow in deprived neighborhoods. Nevertheless, with the development of new goals and a broadened sense of the attainable, library potential is limited only by the vision, time, and energy of its representatives.

The Bushwick Branch Bash

Bessie Bullock
Senior Community Coordinator

Two or three years of working in the Williamsburgh-Bushwick area of Brooklyn as a community coordinator had taught me about the community, the people, and the role, or position, of the library in the day-to-day stream of affairs. I knew that there were many organizations, and less formally organized groups, which worked to improve the community, to solve problems of various kinds, and to give direction and meaning to the energies and interests of their constituents. I knew that there were many individuals who, within or without the framework of organized groups, were keenly aware of trends, were civic-minded, library-minded, and in possession of talents and abilities which were either not widely known or were given little opportunity to be shared with others. I knew, too, that while the library was known and used by many devoted patrons and considered by them to be a mainstay of community life, there were hundreds more who did not have this awareness; indeed, they still stood a bit in awe of THE LIBRARY and were reluctant to explore its physical plant and resources. What could we do that might bring these diverse elements—people, civic structure, and library—closer together? How could we demonstrate their need of, and interdependence upon, one another? How could we sell the library and at the same time make people more aware of their own worth and potential in community life?

Out of these considerations the 13-14 June 1968 "Bushwick Bash" was born. I envisioned an activity predicated on the basic idea of an old-fashioned country fair, where, if one were present at the right time, something very special could be seen and enjoyed, but no matter <u>what</u> time one came, there would be something to savor, to experience, to enjoy. This would be an activity not done <u>by</u> the library <u>to</u> the people <u>for</u> the people, but <u>with</u> the people. Their part would be the "front-line chorus," with the library serving primarily as staging or production agent. While books and other media and resources would be on hand, little emphasis would be put on book borrowing; the stress would be on the library as a many-faceted community agency and a "fun place," where patrons and potential patrons could have a moment in the spotlight. Here would be a time when special talents could be played up and shared with others—in short, this would be a meeting of library and community on a basis not tried before.

The response to this proposed activity was phenomenal. Everybody wanted to get into the act; many whom we approached not only agreed to help, but suggested others who could contribute in some way. What I had originally considered as a project of a half day or so quickly mushroomed into a full two-day Bash, with something by and for everyone of all ages. For example, a small live-plant exhibit by a nine-year-old boy was at one end of the scale, with exhibits, a play, and folk dancing by senior citizens (some in their eighties) at the other. People were quickly and enthusiastically enmeshed in the general idea, and were eager to participate. Other ideas and suggestions were rained upon me from all sides, and I found myself being swept along on the crest of a near-tidal wave of cooperation, interest, and anticipation.

We wanted the Bash—what better way to describe it?—to be held before school closed and the youngsters scattered for the vacation months, so we planned for the month of June and adopted as our slogan "Make It a Library Summer." The library purchased a large banner, in our library colors, proclaiming this slogan, to be hung across the front of the Bushwick Branch; red weather balloons were purchased through a magazine ad, imprinted with the slogan and BPL, inflated, and flown from the roof of the building.

A staff member, Mrs. Pocahontas Harris, suggested a contest to culminate in the crowning of a Prince and Princess Bushwick on the opening day of the Bash. She drew up a plan and rules, and obtained the assistance of community members who interviewed contestants and served as judges in the choice of the winners. The coronation proved to be one of the highlights of the Bash, with youngsters from various schools in the area on hand, along with some parents, to root vigorously for their favorites. Major Owens, a former Brooklyn Public Library community coordinator and now commissioner of the Community Development Agency of New York City, performed the crowning rites.

A street that we had wanted to have closed to traffic for the period of the Bash could not be blocked off because of its proximity to a fire station. However, the Police Department cooperated by giving us "No Parking" privileges for the area in front of and beside the library, except for those vehicles participating in the activities. The local precinct also assigned a patrolman to be on duty at the library for the hours of the Bash. Happily, no untoward incidents took place, but it was comforting to know that the policeman was there if needed.
The New York City Department of Commerce and Industry issued us permits for a street fair and gave us much needed advice and aid along these lines.

A housing project adjacent to the library permitted us to use a playground and grassy area for some of our outdoor activities—the same area was utilized for others that "outgrew" the auditorium space—and further cooperated by lending us a large refrigerator for some of the food that was a part of the festivities. The manager served as a lecturer on black history and drew large audiences. When our own facilities proved too small for the large crowd that came to enjoy the performance of <u>Hansel and Gretel</u> by the senior citizens, an elementary school across the street from the library gave us the use of its auditorium.

Governmental agencies, such as the Fire Department, the local Social Security Office, and various groups under the aegis of the New York City Welfare Department, pledged to participate; other organizations, such as the League of Women Voters, Drug Addiction Programs, Community Action Centers, Neighborhood Coordinating Councils, the American Society for the Prevention of Cruelty to Animals, the Community Center, and so on, all agreed to take part. Many individuals indicated their willingness to cooperate, among them a milliner, a petshop owner, glassblower, kite maker, wood-block printmaker, novelty makers, artists, and several cooks—one a male teacher in a parochial school. Each of the cooks demonstrated the preparation of a specialty and gave out samples for the audiences to enjoy. Included in this latter group were several Puerto Rican women who shared various regional dishes with the audience to the delight of all, adults as well as children. Some women and men who lived in the neighborhood served as hostesses and hosts, helping to direct the visitors, safeguarding some of the exhibits, and generally assisting in whatever way they could.

The end results were more than worth all the effort that went into producing the Bash. In spite of heavy rains on one day, an estimated 7,000 persons of all ages and from different parts of the city attended the activities and went away with a better attitude toward the library. From every side came offers "to help you if you do something like this again" and pleas to "please let's do this again!" As one little boy, with a wide-eyed, open-mouthed look around, exclaimed, "This is a real bash! Gee, we oughta do it every day!" Certainly, the Bushwick Bash proved that library and community not only can work together effectively, but can have real fun doing it.

Appendix

Materials Selection Policy of the Brooklyn Public Library

As a community institution, the public library is dedicated to the concept of service to everyone. A fundamental part of this service is the selection of appropriate materials, which depends, essentially, on four factors:

  I. The objectives of the library.

  II. The community served.

  III. The structure of the library system.

  IV. The nature and quality of the material.

In discussing the relationship of these factors, the purpose of this Materials Selection Policy is to articulate the role of the library in the community and provide guidelines for the staff in their role as selectors.

I. **THE OBJECTIVES OF THE LIBRARY AS FACTORS IN SELECTION**

The Brooklyn Public Library acquires, makes available, and encourages the use of materials in all media which:

Help people know more about themselves and their world.

Supplement formal study and encourage informal self-education.

Meet the informational needs of the entire community.

Stimulate thoughtful participation in the affairs of the community, the country and the world.

Give access to a variety of opinions on matters of current interest and encourage freedom of expression.

Support educational, civic and cultural activities within the community.

Aid in learning and improving job-related skills.

Assist the individual to grow intellectually and spiritually and to enjoy life more fully.

Free and convenient access to the world of ideas, information and the creative experience is of vital importance to every citizen today. The Brooklyn Public Library, therefore, incorporates as part of this policy the Library Bill of Rights, adopted by the Council of the American Library Association, June 27, 1967, and the Freedom to Read Statement, prepared by the Westchester Conference of the American Library Association and the American Book Publisher's

Council, May 2 and 3, 1953. Since the library's concern is the communication of ideas and information, these statements are extended for the purpose of this policy to include all material, in any format.

The library acquires:

1. Source materials and thoughtful interpretations which document and illuminate the past.

2. Contemporary materials representing various points of view, which are of current interest and possible future significance, including materials which reflect current conditions, trends and controversies.

3. Materials designed to increase the individual's ability to function effectively as a productive member of society.

4. Materials which provide a meaningful aesthetic experience, stimulate the imagination and increase the individual's potential for creativity.

5. Materials, including the experimental or controversial, which extend the individual's capacity to understand the world in which he lives.

6. Materials which entertain and which enhance the individual's enjoyment of life.

In a world in which change is so rapid and pervasive, the library's obligation extends beyond meeting present conditions. The library must also strive to anticipate future needs of the community. Books have always been, and will continue to be, a proper concern of the library, but ever greater amounts of information are now being contained in other forms. As research continues in the field of communication, and as the community changes and develops, the library must be a media center, acquiring appropriate materials, regardless of form, and integrating each into its total services.

II.   THE COMMUNITY AS A FACTOR IN SELECTION

The prime factors in the community which have a direct bearing upon the selection of materials are: the people, individually and collectively, and the adequacy and availability of materials in other community agencies.

1. The People

The Brooklyn Public Library serves almost three million people. Although the numerical population of the borough has not changed substantially in the past two decades, the nature of the community is changing. There is ever widening contrast between the stable and the unsettled, the affluent and the poor, the student and the dropout. In this time of rising expectation and deepening frustration, tension and conflict, reflected in every aspect of the urban crisis, the community has enormous needs, both expressed and unexpressed. The variety and scope of materials required by such a community, for information, relaxation, stimulation and education, is as broad as the community itself.

There is an ever-increasing number of college and university students and graduates whose needs for sophisticated materials will continue to be met. In addition, special purpose materials are required to meet the special needs of segments of the population which have not traditionally been library users. The library will continually search for new and better methods and materials in various media and languages to meet these needs.

2. Other Community Resources

The library cooperates as fully as possible with other libraries and with community agencies, groups and organizations whose purposes and activities are related to library objectives. Expanding techniques of interlibrary loan on a city, state and federal level will be utilized to improve service to Brooklyn Public Library patrons. In addition, in order to avoid unnecessary duplication of materials, one factor in selection will be a consideration of the kinds of materials available to the public through other institutions. These include:

a. Special Libraries - Other libraries in the community where materials are available for public or professional use will affect the selection of materials in specialized subject areas. Although materials in all fields will be evaluated for purchase by the library, established special collections are considered the primary sources for professional needs. Purchase of expensive or specialized materials contained in collections like those of The Kings County Medical Society, The New York Academy of Medicine, The Brooklyn Museum, The Brooklyn Botanic Garden, The Long Island Historical Society is generally avoided.

b. Educational Institutions- Cooperation with the entire educational community is a basic aspect of public library service. Responsibility for the provision of curriculum-related materials belongs properly to the schools, but the public library will provide materials which supplement and enrich the reference, research, and recreational needs of student borrowers of all ages. Because of expanding student populations, changing school patterns, revised curricula and developing school libraries, the selection of materials will vary according to the effectiveness with which student requirements are being met by other facilities. The same general standards of merit and relevance that apply to all selection will be used to evaluate curriculum-related materials. Extensive duplication to meet mass assignment demands is not feasible, but through the provision of materials in inexpensive formats (pamphlets, paperbacks, periodicals, etc.) the library will attempt to fill some of the gaps which may ultimately be filled by school and academic libraries as they are developed toward adequacy.

Increasingly, agencies and groups, other than schools and universities, are becoming involved in the educational process. The library will support such activities not only through the provision of its materials and services, but whenever possible by cooperating in the development of appropriate materials and programs.

c. Facilities for the Blind and Visually Handicapped - In cooperation with the New York Public Library's Library for the Blind, service is provided for the blind and visually handicapped in Brooklyn through agencies of the Brooklyn Public Library.

III. THE STRUCTURE OF THE LIBRARY AS A FACTOR IN SELECTION

Within budgetary and space restrictions there are several internal factors which have a direct bearing on the selection of materials. These include the content of the present collection, special interest collections and the structure of the library system.

The Brooklyn Public Library is a network of interdependent agencies and collections designed to make its total resources readily available and widely accessible. Selection of materials will vary according to the function and location of specific agencies. These range from the extensive and specialized collections assembled in the Ingersoll Library to the small, flexible collections of the traveling bookmobiles and vans. Between these two extremes lie a variety of neighborhood libraries different in budget, size and services, but all geared toward meeting the needs of their particular communities. The research collections housed at Ingersoll, the specialized materials and services of the Business Library and the ready reference sources selected for the Telephone Reference Division provide service on a borough and city wide basis. The Ingersoll and Business Library collections include source materials for research and extensive reference collections. These collections are strengthened to the fullest possible extent with a wide range of potentially useful bibliographic aids and encyclopedic works in many languages.

The resources of all library agencies are interlocked via the Interbranch Loan Service, through which any circulating book in the system is made available at any local agency upon request by a borrower. An interlibrary loan arrangement also enables the library to draw upon materials in certain other libraries in the state.

IV. THE NATURE AND QUALITY OF THE MATERIAL AS FACTORS IN SELECTION

Expanding areas of knowledge, changing social values, technological advances and cultural differences require flexibility, open mindedness and responsiveness in the evaluation and re-evaluation of all library materials, old and new. Newspapers, paperbacks, magazines, pamphlets, foreign language materials, films, recordings and other developing types of materials are acquired and made accessible as they are judged suitable, meaningful and relevant to the community.

Materials for Ingersoll's foreign language collection are selected according to the same criteria used for other materials. This collection is available to agencies throughout the system to meet the major needs of the borough. When particular community requirements for foreign language materials cannot be met satisfactorily by the Ingersoll collection, individual agencies will acquire appropriate materials for their own collections.

Each type of material must be considered in terms of its own kind of excellence and the audience for who it is intended. There is no single standard which can be applied in all cases when making an acquisition decision. Some materials may be judged primarily in terms of artistic merit, scholarship or their value as human documents; others are selected to satisfy the recreational and entertainment needs of the community.

A small proportion of the materials evaluated are subject to widespread and/or heavy local demand. Items having such demand may or may not meet the general and specific criteria contained in this policy. In either case the volume and nature of requests by members of the public will be give serious consideration. In addition, as the social and intellectual climate of the community changes, materials which originally were not recommended for purchase may become of interest. Such materials will be re-evaluated on a continuing basis.

To build collections of merit and significance, materials will be considered according to objective guidelines. All acquisitions, whether purchased or donated, are considered in terms of the following standards.

GENERAL CRITERIA:

1. Suitability of physical form for library use.
2. Suitability of subject and style for intended audience.
3. Present and potential relevance to community needs.
4. Appropriateness and effectiveness of medium to content.
5. Insight into human and social condition.
6. Importance as a document of the times.
7. Relation to existing collection and other material on subject.
8. Reputation and/or significance of author.
9. Skill, competence and purpose of author.
10. Attention of critics, reviewers and public.

SPECIFIC CRITERIA FOR THE EVALUATION OF WORKS OF INFORMATION AND OPINION:

1. Authority.
2. Comprehensiveness and depth of treatment.
3. Objectivity.
4. Clarity, accuracy and logic of presentation.
5. Representation of challenging, though extreme or minority point of view.

SPECIFIC CRITERIA FOR THE EVALUATION OF WORKS OF IMAGINATION:

1. Representation of important movement, genre, trend or national culture.
2. Vitality and originality.
3. Artistic presentation and experimentation.
4. Sustained interest.
5. Effective characterization.
6. Authenticity of historical or social setting.

RESPONSIBILITY FOR SELECTION

Using criteria listed above, materials are reviewed by all professional staff. Selection Committees, appointed by the Director supervise and coordinate the entire selection procedure. The final responsibility for selection resides with the Director of the Library.

Append: Library Bill of Rights and the Freedom to Read Statement.

February 1969